Baby Animals Of The World

Speedy Publishing LLC
40 E. Main St. #1156
Newark, DE 19711

www.speedypublishing.com

Copyright 2014
9781635012545
First Printed November 13, 2014

Baby Animals Facts:

A baby dog is called a "pup" or "puppy".

Baby Animals Facts:

A baby cat is called a "kitty" or "kitten".

Baby Animals Facts:

Polar bears usually only have two cubs and they have these babies in a cave they've dug in a large snow drift. They stay there over winter and come out in spring with the babies.

Baby Animals Facts:

Polar bear babies are much smaller than human babies when they're born. They are the size of a rat and weigh little more than a pound. They can grow to full man size in a year if they have lots of food.

Baby Animals Facts:

A baby monkey is called an "infant". A group of monkeys is called a "troop."

Baby Animals Facts:

Tiger cubs mature quickly. At 8 weeks old, they are ready to learn how to hunt and go out on hunting expeditions with their mother.

Baby Animals Facts:

The name for a male Guinea pig is a 'boar', the name for a female Guinea pig is a 'sow'. A baby guinea pig is called a 'pup'.

Baby Animals Facts:

After mating, female foxes will make a nest of leaves inside her burrow on which to have her pups. This special room in the burrow is called a nesting chamber.

Baby Animals Facts:

When the pups are born, they are cared for by all of the adult wolves in the pack. Young pups start off drinking milk from their mother, but around five to 10 weeks they will start eating food regurgitated from adult pack members.

Baby Animals Facts:

Lions are very social compared to other cat species, often living in prides that feature females, offspring and a few adult males.

Baby Animals Facts:

Baby seals, called pups, will stay on land until their waterproof fur grows in. This can take around a month.

Baby Animals Facts:

Mothers carry their young for a gestation period of around 10 months. Seals and sea lions have just one pup a year.

Baby Animals Facts:

When penguin chicks are ready to hatch, they use their beaks to break through the shell of their eggs. This process can take up to three days.

Baby Animals Facts:

After the chicks emerge, the parents will take turns feeding their offspring with regurgitated food. Penguin parents can identify their offspring by unique calls that the chick will make.

Baby Animals Facts:

A baby elephant is called a calf. As the calf grows, it will gain 2 to 3 lbs. every day until its first birthday.

Baby Animals Facts:

Baby zebras are called foals. Soon after birth, foals are able to stand up and walk.

Baby Animals Facts:

Baby rabbits are called kittens or kits. After four to five weeks, a kit can care for itself. In two or three months it is ready to start a family of its own.

Baby Animals Facts:

A young deer is usually called a 'fawn'. Most deer are born with white spots but lose them within a year.

Baby Animals Facts:

At birth, the baby kangaroo, called a joey, can be as small as a grain of rice, or as big as a bee, at 0.2 to 0.9 inches (5 to 25 millimeters). When the joey is born, it is guided safely into the comfy pouch, where it gestates for another 120 to 450 days.

Made in the USA
Middletown, DE
13 January 2016